T0158059

JOURNEYS OF THREE GENERATIONS

From China, America, Hawaii

A True Story By
Barbara Yuen O'Connor

Inspiring Voices®
A Service of **Guideposts**

Inspiring Voices books may be ordered through booksellers or by contacting:

Inspiring Voices
1663 Liberty Drive
Bloomington, IN 47403
www.inspiringvoices.com
1 (866) 697-5313

ISBN: 978-1-4624-0936-5 (sc)
ISBN: 978-1-4624-0937-2 (e)

Library of Congress Control Number: 2014905879

Printed in the United States of America.

Inspiring Voices rev. date: 03/26/2014

CONTENTS

ACKNOWLEDGMENTS

I want to thank our Doctors for all they did for Frank and to my Hospice friends helping me through my pain and grief.

And to my friends and family that helped and encouraged me throughout my life to become the person I am today. A positive person full of hope and faith.

CHAPTER ONE

GRANDFATHER

This is about three generations of an Asian-American family. When my husband died I was filled with grief. We were married 39 years and I couldn't believe he was gone. At the suggestion of my dog's vet, I decided to attend a hospice grief support group. Five weeks after he died I attended my first meeting. At one of the sessions a suggestion was made that we write about the memories we shared with our spouse. I began to think it was a good idea but why only my spouse? Why not all of my loved ones I had lost? So, I'm writing about my grandparents, parents, and myself. At this hospice grief group I met men and women with whom I identified. They also had a difficult time with losing a loved one. I bonded with several of them and felt fortunate to have found this group.

Let me start with my grandparents. My grandfather was born in Ping Tong Village in China in the year 1857. He received money for passage from relatives and his district association. He stepped out with faith and hope in his heart. He left China on a steamship and sailed to America when he was 20 years old. When he arrived in America he said his name was Chun AhPing. His first name was AhPing and last name was Chun. Somehow his last name Chun became his first name and AhPing became his last name. He arrived in the United Sates in the year 1877 before the Chinese Exclusion Act of 1882. He remained in San Francisco for a year working on the railroads as a laborer.

During this period in history there was a great deal of discrimination against the Chinese immigrants.

Grandfather AhPing Chun

The Chinese Exclusion Act was signed into law in 1882, halted Chinese immigration for ten years and prohibited the Chinese from becoming US citizens. There were several acts following the 1882 act. The act of 1929 capped overall immigration to the US at 150.000 per year and barred Asian immigration. This law was repealed by another act in 1943 during World War II when China was an ally in the war against Japan. After 80 years it was the 1943 act which allowed them to migrate to the United States.

The Chinese immigrants were not welcomed. However, this did not discourage my grandfather. In 1878 he signed a three year contract with other Chinese laborers to work in Hawaii's growing sugar industry. He spent most of his life on the island of Maui and Molokai. Upon his arrival he and fifteen of his countrymen worked on a sugar plantation on Molokai. When he arrived he found only two Chinese men on the island. Life was simple but hard. My grandfather was very industrious and managed to survive and progress through sheer hard work. After two years at the plantation he and the others were asked to leave because the owners were closing down the plantation due to financial difficulties. Since they were under contract, they tried to get the owners to provide promised passage to return to California. Since they were unable to receive funds to return to California my Grandfather and the others left Molokai to seek employment on the other islands. One of his friends remained on the island, purchased property and opened a store.

Grandfather left Molokai to work on the Puunene Sugar Plantation on Maui where he was employed as camp cook for five years. After working for the Puunene Sugar Plantation, he went to Kipahulu to work as a plantation overseer. Grandfather remained in this capacity for ten years until he was transferred to Lahaina where he continued as an overseer. After 5 years at Lahaina, he returned to work at Kipahulu as the manager for the Kipahulu Sugar Plantation. The plantation was losing money until my grandfather took over. He worked at this plantation for nine years. In 1915 when the owner sold the plantation, he decided to relocate his family to Honolulu. He had saved his money and wanted to retire early.

While he was working in Maui, he went back to China to visit his parents. During his stay in the islands, he made two trips back to China. His first trip in 1899 his parents found him a bride. He married my grandmother in the traditional Chinese custom.

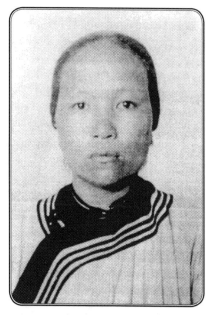

Grandmother/Bride

When they returned to the islands, he married her again the American way. They lived on Maui and had fourteen children. One set of the children were twins and my grand-mother lost them in childbirth. They raised four boys and eight girls in Maui and Honolulu. The majority of the family was born on Maui which was part of the Territory of Hawaii. The islands of Hawaii did not become a state until 1959. Two of the younger children were born in Honolulu. According to my mother, living conditions were both hard for the children as well as their parents. The children would have to share beds and wore hand me down clothes. However, they were never without food or love. She said that she and her siblings always enjoyed Chinese New Year because they would have new shoes and clothes. They looked forward for this festival. New Years is a festival that the Chinese enjoyed celebrating.

Family

In 1912, Grandfather and Grandmother took their family to China to visit his 87 years old mother. They were in China for a short time. While in China, Grandfather built a school to help educate the children of his village. There were frequent night robberies so he also acted as a night watchman for the village. When they were leaving China, one of their daughters loved her grandmother so much she did not return to the islands with her family. My mother and the rest of the family returned to Maui where the majority of the children grew up. The family completely lost track of this daughter that they left in China.

The family lived in Maui until 1915. My grandfather retired and moved his family to Honolulu. He had saved his money and bought a hotel in Honolulu. His oldest son remained on the island of Maui and opened a poi factory. The rest of the family lived in Honolulu. He bought the Nuuanu Hotel with the intention of retiring. His friend on Molokai, that opened a store, told my grandfather he was getting old and needed help with his store. He offered my grandfather a great opportunity. The family could move to Molokai and live on his property. He had no family and told my grandfather when he died the store and property would be left to him.

In 1921 he took his friend's offer and relocated his family. After his friend's death, he operated this merchandise store with two of his older sons. In memory of his friend he dedicated a portion of the property for a cemetery. His friend was the first person to be buried there. The majority of the customers that patronized the store were Hawaiians. My grandfather spoke Chinese, English and Hawaiian. He learned English from the missionaries and Hawaiian from his Hawaiian customers. He loved and had faith in his customers so much he lent money to many of them to build or repair their homes. When they couldn't pay for their merchandise,

7

he would allow them to charge their merchandise. He had a strange way of bookkeeping. Nothing was kept on paper. Everything was kept in his head. He used an abacus which is a Chinese adding machine. When he died at 93 years old, his sons had no idea who owed the store money. Many came forward to let my uncles know grandfather had helped them and they wanted to repay their debt.

While my grandfather worked at the store, my grandmother kept the house and children. She planted fruit trees, raised hogs, chickens and pigeons. She planted her own vegetables. Her trees included avocado, macadamia nuts, papaya, banana, mango, limes and lychee. She planted peanuts which she would boil or roast and sold in the store. Her boiled peanuts were a popular item. She sold her fruits in the store. She started with one tree in her orchard in 1925, ended with 80 or more trees. She loved to work outdoors and did all the work herself.

I remember as a child there was a wood burning stove in the kitchen which she used to prepare the family meals. She not only cooked on this stove but she used the oven to bake us bread and pies. She was a marvelous cook. A pot of black tea was available in the kitchen any time of the day. This was a familiar sight in most Asian households. Grandmother died before her husband at the age of 82. Towards the end of their lives they both became Christians. They both lived through the depression years by working hard, helping others and never losing faith. They loved the islands. They were thankful to have had the opportunity to leave China and live in such a wonderful country.

Also, while living with my Grandparents and parents our primary language was English. My Grandparents spoke English with some Hawaiian words mixed in their sentences to their grandchildren. Although my parents spoke Chinese and a little Hawaiian we spoke only English in our home. My parents said English should be the primary language if you live in Hawaii. I regret that they did not teach me the Chinese language.

I didn't learn to use chopsticks until I graduated from high school. I was invited to a Chinese party at a restaurant and had to ask for a fork. I was asked by a Caucasian woman who was using chopsticks, "Do you not like using chopsticks?" I replied, "I have a difficult time using them". I didn't tell her the truth. We didn't use chopsticks in our home and I never had the desire to use them. You can't pick up too much food with them. When I went home I told my mother about this incident and had lessons on how to pick up food with two small thin sticks.

Two of the older sons remained with their parents and the youngest son left the islands with his other sisters. One of the older sons married the daughter of the owner of a sugar plantation. This was the same plantation owner who employed grandfather to work on his plantation when he first arrived on Molokai from San Francisco. The daughters went to Honolulu to find jobs or go to school. Several of them got married, others worked in sales and one went to college to become a teacher.

My mother remained with her parents. She was 19 years old when she married my father and he was 20 years old. The matchmaker's for her marriage was my mother's parents and my father's older brother. The process of matchmaking is a Chinese tradition of choosing a spouse between two families. When the two families agree to the marriage the man's family is supposed to send some betrothal gifts to the woman's family. My grandparents received money (in the form of gold coins), chickens, and hogs. Before I was born God had picked my parents. My parents were married and after a year they had me and named me Barbara. My father's parents left the islands to live in Shanghai. Both were killed in a raid by the Japanese in 1937.

My father worked for his older brother as a manager in one of his brother's stores. Father had four brothers. Two of his brothers had opened general stores. Another was a lawyer and his younger brother got the franchise for Frito Lay. He opened a potato chip factory in Honolulu. My grandfather's store was on the east side of the island and my father's brother had stores on the west side of the island. My mother stayed home to take care of me and the house. Life as a child was good. I had everything. I was the only child but my parents were very strict. I remember one Halloween day my father came home early. He wanted to know if I had done my home work which I had not done. He told me that he was going to go through the questions with me. One of the questions he asked me was who lived in the White House. I told him ghosts. I knew the answer but I thought my answer was funny. He didn't think it was funny. He told me that I would not be able to go trick or treating that night. I thought all was going well with my parents. I had no idea this all would end.

Father would come home late and his excuse was that he was busy at the store. The bickering between my parents became worse as the months came and went. Mother found out he was seeing another woman. She told him he either had to quit seeing this woman or she was leaving him. He made the choice of leaving us. He started seeing this other woman after my mother lost their baby in a car accident. We would visit my grandparents every Sunday. One Sunday afternoon, as we were going around a curve a car collided with our vehicle. No one was hurt seriously in the other car, however, my mother and I were seriously injured and were air lifted to Honolulu. She had a miscarriage and I had a broken jaw. I also lost a great deal of blood. Instead of drawing closer to each other, they grew apart which ended with my father leaving us. After he left us he never tried to contact me. At the age of 7, I learned that life wasn't easy. When he made the choice to leave us, we packed up and left my comfortable life to live with my grandparents.

It was fun living with them. Animals to feed and a store with lots of soda pop, crackers and I won't forget the candy. I loved being with my grandmother and grandfather. I admired them. They worked hard to raise their family and were living during the depression years. I never heard them complain or get discouraged. I remember my mother and me helping my grandmother with picking fruits and peanuts. These were wonderful times in my life.

My parents did not get back together. They separated and my father never helped my mother financially. Our life changed drastically. Mother became a single parent with a child to support. She had never worked nor been on her own so this was a new experience.

We lived with her parents for a year then mother decided she had to get a life of her own and move on. Her younger sister who lived on another island needed help caring for her new born son. Since she wanted to go back to work she needed someone she could trust to take care of him. She and her husband agreed they would let mother and I stay with them in exchange for my mother's help. I went to school and my mother took care of the baby. When I came home from school, I helped her with baby sitting. While I took care of the baby she did the cooking, washing and house cleaning.

After leaving the home of my grandparents, my mother and I would be living with one relative or another. When the baby was older, we left my mother's younger sister's house to live with another one of her sisters. This was Katherine her older sister. She was a school teacher, single and had bought a three bedroom house. She wanted mother to live in the city where she could find a job. She was hired by the YWCA as a housekeeper. Since both my mom and Katherine were working, they didn't want me to be at home alone. They decided the safest and best place for me was in a boarding school. My auntie Katherine said she would help my mother with the tuition. So at the beginning of the school year in September 1941, I was placed in a Christian boarding school.

At school things were going good until Sunday morning, December 7, 1941. There was a great deal of commotion in the hallway in our dormitory. We wondered what was going on. We were on our way for breakfast and chapel service. We ran outside to see what was happening and heard loud explosion sounds and black smoke in the sky in the location of Pearl Harbor. Someone announced that Pearl Harbor was being bombed by the Japanese. After breakfast and a prayer meeting, we were informed that our parents were contacted to take us home. The school was being turned into a hospital to accommodate the other hospitals. My mother and her sister did not drive. Mother had to either get a taxi or catch the bus. She was unable to locate a taxi and took a bus. I gathered all my belongings and waited for her. Finally we arrived home safely.

I remember the black outs we had to observe in our home. The bomb shelter the three of us had dug in the backyard of our house. We had air raid drills in school. Gas masks were issued which we took to school. Food and gas were rationed. United States currency used in the islands had Hawaii printed on them. The reason for this was in the event the Japanese captured the islands they would not be able to use this currency.

In 1944 the boarding school that I attended before December 7, 1941 opened up to boarders. The war brought many servicemen to the islands. Many changes were taking place. My mother quit her job at the YWCA and worked for her friend in an arcade center for servicemen. She was a mother and sister to sailors, marines and soldiers who were away from their families. When she started to work at this new job, both she and my Auntie said to me one day "We are sending you back to the school you attended before the attack on Pearl Harbor". I said to them "I want to attend the school I'm attending and I don't want to leave my friends". I was outnumbered and sent back to the boarding school. Since they were both working, they said "We don't want to leave you home alone. We want you where we know you will be safe". Both girls and boys attended this school. I attended this school my freshmen through my senior year.

Summer vacations were spent on Molokai with my grandparents. I remember how my grandfather would come home from the store to listen to the news on the war. Whenever the Americans, British, and Russians were advancing and were winning he would shout and clap his hands. My grandparents were glad when the war ended. Their youngest son, who was drafted into the army, came home safe. The last summer I was with them I received a gift of a U.S. savings bond for working at the store. In all the summers I spent on Molokai I never once saw my father. When I graduated from high school, I sent him an invitation but he did not attend. After I graduated my mother divorced my father.

During my years at school, I learned how to handle and take care of myself. I washed and ironed my clothes. I learned how to manage the allowance my mother gave me each month. The school allowed us to go home once a month on weekends. I enjoyed these weekends. This Christian school had a great influence on my life. I learned how to be independent.

We started each day with breakfast, chapel service and classes. After dinner we had study hall and lights out at 9:00 P.M. Saturday events were attending a movie or a dance. The girls were excited whenever dances were scheduled. Talking about gowns they were purchasing or wearing. I never took part in these conversations because I knew exactly what I was wearing. I had two gowns I wore for four years and I wasn't crazy about going to these dances. I was fat and unattractive and was never asked for a dance by the boys. I sat with the other unattractive girls until it was time to return to our dorm. I studied real hard and had good grades. I wanted to go to college but I knew it would be hard on our finances.

While I was still attending school, my Auntie sold her house to move in with another sister who lost her husband and lived alone. My mother and I went to live with her sister-in-law who had a large house and a daughter and son. Her husband, my mother's brother, worked and lived with his parents on Molokai.

CHAPTER TWO
MY BANKING CAREER

After graduation I decided I would put off going to college. I told my mother I was going to work and later go to college. She was against this decision. She said "I want you to go to college because I didn't have the opportunity. You have the opportunity to do something I wasn't able to do". "Mom I don't want you to work anymore to support both of us. It's my turn to support us" I said. I found a job in a bank after I graduated. It was a job in the bookkeeping department. The timing was perfect because the war was ending and the job my mother had would eventually end. She quit her job and I went to work. College had to wait.

While working at the bank I met a number of good people. They were nice and kind. I was 18 years old and this was a new experience. I never worked before except during the war when one day a month the school would load us on buses to go to the pineapple fields to harvest pineapples. Several of the men that worked in the fields joined the armed forces and the pineapples needed to be harvested. Working in the pineapple fields was hard work. We had to walk between the rows of pineapple with a large burlap bag over our shoulders. As we picked the fruit to put in the bags, we were continually poked by the sharp pineapple leaves. We were helping with the war effort and were being paid .25 cents an hour by the pineapple company. I bought .25 cent savings war stamps with my money. I had a booklet which I pasted the stamps in and when I got it filled I was able to buy an $18.75 savings bond.

From the bookkeeping department I was promoted to teller. Being a teller you meet a number of business men and women. One day while I was having a conversation with one of them, he said "Know anyone that wants to rent an apartment?" I said "Yes me". I asked him for the location and the rental amount. I wanted to be sure that I could afford the rent. Since the rent was $110.00 a month, I was able to afford it. My mother and I moved into the apartment. For the first time in our lives we were not living with relatives and we were so happy.

Working in the banking industry, I learned to never judge a person by the way they dressed or how they look. For several years I waited on a customer who owned apartments and a Laundromat that used coin operated machines for washing and drying clothes. My counter was close to the entrance and he would come to me with his unwrapped coins. The coins had to be sorted, placed in coin wrappers and an account number had to be on each of them. Some of the tellers would say to me "Why don't you give him the wrappers and let him know the coins should be wrapped?" I replied "I'm sure none of you would make that remark to him". He very seldom went to anyone else because my counter was near the entrance. The bank president was retiring and the directors of the bank were looking for a replacement. One of the employees said, "Guess who will be our next president". It was the customer that I had waited on for over a year. Later he became the bank's CEO. I learned from this experience. Do not judge people on what they do for a living or how they dress. One day they might become your boss. Treat everyone with respect. He promoted me as the bank's first woman officer. Later he promoted another woman to take over the marketing division. He believed in equal opportunity for women. He paid and treated us like the men. He was very demanding. I was head of the teller's department. I remember at one of our monthly meetings, he said to the woman in marketing "How many new business establishments did you visit this month and how many of them have opened accounts?" She replied "I went to five places and I'm trying to encourage them to move their accounts". He shouted "I want the accounts here now". Also, he used inappropriate language to make his point. After the meeting I met her in the ladies restroom and she was in tears. I decided I was going to seek employment at another establishment. I belonged to a group of women officers from other banks. One of the women I met at one of our conferences was President Obama's grandmother. She was one of the first women officers in her bank. She worked for one of the largest banks on the island. I called her and asked for a job at her bank. She was very accommodating and said "Come over and fill out an application. I'll be glad to help you". However, I decided to seek employment at an Asian American bank across the street from the bank I was employed. It had opened only two years prior to my employment with them. After 16 years at the same company, it was difficult to leave. I was afraid to start over again from the bottom. After searching for the right answer, I came to the conclusion that I should accept the position which was offered to me. I took a cut in salary plus a position as a teller.

A San Francisco trip

Two years later, I was promoted to Head Teller and five years later I became Assistant Vice-President. I was the first woman to hold this position at this bank. Being the only woman officer I had many benefits. I was sent with all expenses paid to conferences with other women bank officers in my area and in the rest of the United States. I enjoyed working for this company. My mother and I were set financially and I felt secure in my job and life was wonderful. I realized you don't have to go to college to get ahead. You need to work hard at what you're doing and have patience and faith. I started out in the financial field as a bookkeeper and ended up as Assistant Vice-President without a college education.

Bank conference

A great many opportunities opened up for me. I learned how to get into the stock market and real estate. The customers of both banks helped me get started with investing in stocks and real estate. The first stock that I purchased was a whiskey stock. One of my customers recommended this stock to me. He told me working at the bank would not provide me with the income I needed. He suggested that I purchase stocks.

I asked him, "What are stocks?" He explained to me what stocks were and he would have his broker call me. "What is a broker?" I asked. I learned what a stock broker was. Now I knew what stocks were and what a stock broker did. I bought the stocks, sold them and made a profit. This was my introduction to the stock market. When I had an opportunity to go into the real estate business, I had to turn it down. Another customer owned a real estate business. One day he said, "I want you to be one of my agents in my real estate company. I will train you to get your license and you can work for my company". I replied "I don't have a car because I don't drive". I knew he would be willing to teach me to drive. I made the following statement "I'm not going to learn how to drive because I'm afraid to drive." I knew you had to have a car and drive to meet clients. So I waited to see what he would say next. He pointed another way to invest in the real estate market and make a profit. He said "You don't need a car or drive. You need a small sum of money". I was interested. After all I had my mother and me to support. I didn't want to pay rent to someone else the rest of our lives. Someday I wanted to purchase a condominium. He knew I had a small amount of cash and he showed me how to make this work for me. He said "You can purchase a beach property on the island you were born for a small down payment of $500.00 on an agreement of sale and $110.00

a month". He explained what an agreement of sale meant. I had no idea what it meant. I told him I would have to discuss this with my mother. After work I went home and told her about this offer. Her answer was "No". After much talking, I finally convinced her it was a good idea. The deal was made with the realtor and we acquired an acre of beach property.

I heard two of the directors of the bank were developing a 24 story condominium. The employees had first preference to make a purchase. If no one was interested, they would put it on the market. I disliked paying rent for our apartment and not having anything to show for it. I decided this was a great opportunity. I hurried home to tell my mother about this opportunity. When I told her about the condo, her answer was "No". I pleaded with her. I said "Please go with me tomorrow and look at this place". She didn't say no. After, work we both went to see the condo. She didn't like the idea of having to get into an elevator to get to your condo. The apartment we were renting was one story. We looked inside the condo. She liked the inside but didn't like living in a high rise. A few of the condos were on the first floor and it wasn't necessary to use the elevator. She was interested in one of the condos on the first floor. The next day I went to work and spoke to one of the directors. I told him we were interested in one of the condos on the first floor. He brought out plans for the condos and said, "Please could you point out on the plans which condo you are interested?" I pointed out the one we wanted. He looked at me and replied, "I'm sorry but this is the condo we had reserved for the manager".

I told him I would go home and let mother know the condo was reserved for the manager. I went home and gave her the news. I tried to change her mind by letting her know there were other condos on the first floor. They had their own entrance and there was no need to use the elevator. She was stubborn and I couldn't change her mind. Her answer was "No if we can't have that condo I don't want us to purchase any of the others". The next day I went to work one of the partners' had discussed my situation with his partner. If I could qualify for a mortgage loan, the condo would be ours. He and his partner agreed they would move the manager to another condo on the first floor. I did qualify for the loan and we moved into our new home.

I don't remember ever doing anything without my mother's consent. After my father left us, it had always been the two of us. I loved my mother. She dated a few times and after awhile she stopped dating. She reminded me we had to take care of each other and never trust anyone. I dated but was never serious with anyone. It was common knowledge in the community I was very close to my mother. Many men didn't want the excess baggage of a mother-in-law. Whenever I thought I was in a serious relationship, I would cut it off. I let it be known that I would never leave my mother. I dated a police officer who had been my friend for 17 years. I felt comfortable with him because I knew he was taking care of his mother and he would never leave her. He felt the same way about his mother as I did about my mother. We had a good relationship.

Mother and Barbara

I felt secure in my job and enjoyed the work. However, my boss found another job and I had a new boss. Things changed. The bank installed their first computers when the computers came out. I worked long hours but I didn't mind. I just didn't like going home on the bus late at night. Sometimes my police friend would pick me up but he worked odd shifts. Often I had to take the bus. One night I was waiting to catch the bus and my boss stopped and offered me a ride home. I took his offer and he was real nice and friendly. Several months went by before he asked me out but I declined. He made it very obvious that he wanted more than a 'boss and employee' relationship. Today, we call it sexual harassment. He was married and was known to be a good family man. This harassment went on for almost a year. I tried to ignore him. I thought of complaining to his superiors but what if they didn't believe me. Matter of fact I knew my superiors would not believe me. During this decade women were portrayed as being wrong in such circumstances. After all he was married plus a good family man. I was single. I needed the job and didn't want to be fired. I felt trapped and wanted to get out of this situation. I didn't know what to do. I couldn't talk to anyone about it.

One day after lunch I took a walk. I walked passed a cathedral called Our Lady of Peace. I don't know what prompted me to walk back and I was drawn into the cathedral. I went in and sat down. Thoughts of how much I needed help ran through my mind. At that time I didn't know who or where the help I needed would come from. When I left, I felt that a great burden was lifted from me.

I went back to work hoping the help I needed would be answered.

When I got back to work, my boss called me into his office. He said to me, "We are opening a new branch office in a month. I want you to help with the opening which will be on a Saturday". I replied "I don't work on Saturdays. It's my day off". He said "I'll be expecting you to be there at 8:00". He told me that after the branch closed lunch would be provided.

On Saturday I was at the branch at 8:00. When the branch closed, lunch was served. The company that built the branch supplied the lunch. After lunch the project manager for this company got up to leave because he had another commitment and had to leave early. My boss looked at me and said, "The man wants to leave let him out." I wanted to say to my boss let him out yourself however, I got up and walked to the door. As I unlocked the door Frank asked "Are you married?" I said "No are you married?" He answered "No". We said goodbye and just for a moment I wondered why he asked me such a question.

A week after the branch opening, I received a call from the branch manager. He asked me if I had gotten a call from the project manager Frank. Frank had called the branch looking for me. The manager told him I worked at the Main Office. The manager said "I gave him the main branches' phone number. After I gave him the number I thought maybe I shouldn't have done that without asking you". I assured him it was okay. He then invited me to a beach party at his beach home. He was inviting the employees who helped him with the opening of his branch. I thanked him for the invitation but told him I couldn't make it. A few days later Frank called. He told me he was invited to the beach party and didn't want to go alone. He asked, "Are you invited to the party?" I replied "I don't drive and I hadn't given it much thought". He said "If you would go with me, I'll be glad to take you". I decided to go to the beach party with him and we had a wonderful time.

On Monday, Frank called and asked me to have dinner with him and I accepted. I found out he was from California and not from the islands. He was very tan and I had thought he was an islander (Hawaiian-Portuguese) with blue eyes. He worked for a company based in Sacramento. He said he would leave the islands when his company finished all their projects and would go to Florida or Alaska to look for work. Frank would pick me up after work on the days I worked late. My boss asked me "Are you going with that haole (white) guy?" I answered "Yes". It was then that my boss got the message. He didn't bother me anymore. It was many years later before I realized in going into the cathedral and praying for help, my prayers were answered and God had put Frank in my life. I would never have met Frank had I refused to work on Saturday at the branch opening. God had a plan in progress for me.

It would be eight months before his company's projects would be finished. He then would be leaving the islands. This didn't bother me. We enjoyed each others company and became good friends. I brought him home to introduce him to my mother. I was surprised that she liked him. Weekends the three of us would pack a picnic lunch and head for the beach. My mother knew Frank eventually would be leaving the islands and was no threat to her.

Several months later, I came home to an upset Mother. No sooner did I set foot in the door when she shouted "Frank said he wanted to marry you and if it was okay with me. If you marry him you will move out of this condo". I replied, "He just dropped me off and never mentioned marriage to me. He is leaving the islands to go to Alaska or Florida to work. You don't have to worry. He hasn't asked me to marry him and if he does ask me I would say no". She calmed down and was satisfied with my answer. It wasn't because Frank was Caucasian that she disapproved of me marrying him, although there was a great deal of racial prejudice during this period in the islands against anyone that was not from the islands. My mother was not prejudiced. She was a controlling and possessive parent. She would never approve of anyone

I married. She may have thought she gave up her life to take care of me and I should do the same for her. Also, she thought no one was good enough for her daughter. There are parents who have these thoughts. Frank had no money and we knew little about him. She told me I had a good life and not to make a grave mistake by losing everything I had worked so hard to achieve. She reminded me of all the trips I had made to the orient and United States. These trips would stop if I got married because I would have a husband and perhaps a family to take care of.

The next day I went to work and told one of my lady friends what had happened. She said, "Bobbie, move out and make a life of your own. You're not a teenager. Don't let her control your life. You're in your 40's". I replied, "It's not that easy. I don't have money to move out and get an apartment of my own. I have no place to go". She said "I can't have you stay with me because I have a family. If I was alone, I would gladly have you stay with me until you could be on your own". She suggested I ask Frank if I could move in with him temporarily until I could afford a place of my own. She said, "He created this mess so ask him for help".

Frank picked me up after work and I confronted him. I said, "Why did you tell my mother that you wanted to marry me and not even ask me first?" She said if I married you I would have to move out of the condo. He replied, "I was waiting for the right time to propose". I asked him about his plans to go to Alaska or Florida. He told me that if we got married he would find work on the islands and would not move. I told him I enjoyed his company and we were good friends but I was not in love with him. Also, I told him about the conversation I had with my friend. She suggested that I move out and be on my own but I had no place to go. I told him she suggested I ask him if I could move in with him until I was able to find a place of my own and sort things out. He said "Yes you should go out on your own and I have a two bedroom apartment. I was going to look for someone to share the apartment until I left the island. You may move in with me until you can find a place of your own". My friend helped me move out of my mother's apartment and I moved in with Frank.

It was difficult for me to save money for an apartment. I needed a deposit plus a one months' rent and I still had the mortgage on my mother's condo and the beach property on Molokai. Frank continually asked me to marry him. During this period it was unacceptable to live with each other and not be married. The community that I had known all my life would defiantly frown on this. And I thought 'what if he decides to leave the island?' If I still did not find a place of my own, I would have to go back and live with my mother I loved her but

I could hear her say, "I told you it wouldn't work out but you wouldn't listen".

The next time he asked me to marry him. My answer was "Yes". Again I told him that I wasn't in love with him. He said, "I love you and I hope someday you will love me". We were married in the office of a judge whom I knew from the bank.

Wedding Day 10-02-71

One of Franks' friend and my friend were our witnesses. A party was given at my friends' house.

My friends and Franks friends were at the party. We invited my family but no one showed up. They had stopped associating with me the day I moved out of my mothers' condo.

Wedding Party

CHAPTER THREE

OUR LIFE TOGETHER

Frank did all the cooking because I didn't know how to cook. My mother did all the cooking when I lived with her. However, I did know how to wash and clean the condo because when I was living with my mother that was my job. Her job was the cooking. After four months I learned how to cook.

We went to our first bank Christmas party in our Datsun pick up. People drove up to the entrance of the club in nice cars. We drove up to the front entrance of the Oahu Country Club in our pick up. The valet parked our pick up and we went to the party. I won a television which we loaded in our pick up truck.

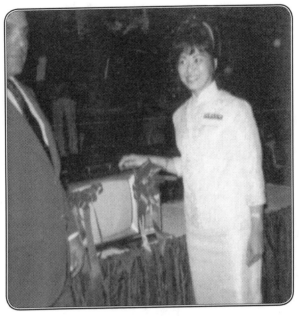

Party won TV

Life with Frank was good and we were very happy. After four months of being married, Frank had a terrible accident at work. This was to completely change our lives. After work, he was boarding up an old building in China town. As he was nailing up a board, a huge drain pipe came loose and fell on his head. It smashed his hard hat so hard it looked like an accordion. It was a miracle he wasn't killed instantly. Frank was rushed to a hospital. The doctor told us two of his vertebras in his back were fractured. The doctor said to Frank and I, "We have no time to lose and have to operate as soon as possible". The operation was done the next day. Frank was in the hospital for almost two weeks. He was told he would not be able to go back to work for five months or more. Things were going so well and wham we were hit with adversity.

We had only my salary to live on. There was rent to pay, doctor bills, and my mother's mortgages. I didn't know how we could manage all these bills. Since Frank got hurt on the job, he could file workers compensation. I told him we had all these bills to pay and he should file workers compensation. His answer was "No". I said "We could stop paying mom's mortgages. This would help us. She has money to make her own payments". Again, "No" was his answer. "We both agreed that when you moved out we would continue to pay her mortgages. We will find someway to get through our problems. This is not your mothers' problem. We will continue to pay her mortgages". When I heard him say these things, I realized I married the right man and how could I not love such a good man. I said to him, "Frank, thank you for reminding me of the agreement we made to pay Mom's mortgages". I told him, I loved him and no matter how hard things were we would be able to work out our finances. He remembered he could qualify for unemployment until he was able to go back to work. During this period we ate hot dogs and a lot of salads.

He was home recuperating while I went to work. After four months, I came home from work to find a machine in the back of our Datsun truck. I asked him "What is that thing in the back of your pick up?" It was a welding machine and he had decided to open a welding shop. He had looked through the yellow pages and found there was a need for a welding shop on the islands. It was too costly to import steel which had to be fabricated in California and shipped to the islands. He was going to fabricate the steel in his shop. I asked him if he had found a location for his shop. The machine was weighing down the truck tires and we were unable to use the truck. He replied, "Don't worry I'll find a shop". I said, "If you find a shop how are you going to unload the machine and can we afford renting a shop?" He was still wearing a back brace and suffered some pain. His replay was "Not to worry."

Several weeks later I came home and the machine was gone. The first thing I said to him when I entered the apartment "Where is the machine?" He had found a shop for $50.00 a month. I wanted to know how he was able to move the machine into the shop. He saw a man with a forklift who was moving lumber into his shop. Frank called out to the man "Hey bro can you help me unload this machine into my shop?" The man helped Frank unload the welding machine. We thought what a coincidence. The man was there at the right time and place. Many years later we knew better. People who come into our lives were not put there by coincidence. God had a hand sending these earth angels to us. If there are angels in heaven, we certainly have angels among us on earth.

A few days later Frank set up his shop. He bought welding supplies he would need. He knew we were on a budget so he was very prudent in his purchases. His first job came a month later. It was from the company he was employed by when he got hurt and wouldn't file worker's compensation. They put in an order for three truck racks. Later, we had contracts from them to fabricate angles, steel beams and other items.

Start of the new shop

New shop getting busy!

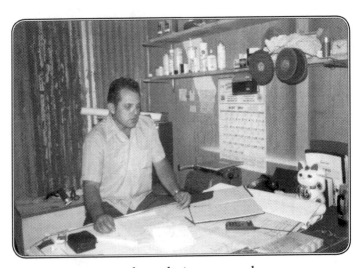

Frank pondering new work

We could not afford to hire anyone. It took us six to eight months before he was able to hire two men to help him. He had so much work to turn out and one person wasn't able to do it alone. We had saved enough to make payroll. There were times when we thought we couldn't meet our payroll and then we would receive a check from one of our customers for the amount to pay our suppliers and meet our payroll. Was this just another coincidence we asked ourselves? The more we talked about the subject the more we knew it wasn't a coincidence.

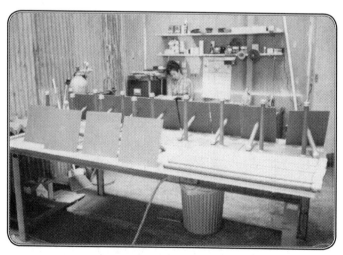

After work I would go to the shop to help

A year later, we moved to another apartment and about a block from our new apartment was a church. We went by this church for several months but had no desire to go in. One Sunday we decided we would attend this church. The pastor preached a powerful sermon. His sermon changed our lives forever. We both were baptized in this church. We learned that the obstacles in our life were put there for a reason. Obstacles and adversities are to make us strong for other disasters and God puts people in our lives to help us through them.

Frank's shop was doing very well. He hired more men and started to fabricate sewage treatment tanks for the outside island hotels. I remember the first tank they fabricated could not be loaded on the barge that went to Maui. The stevedores at the dock would not load the tank because it was fabricated by a non-union shop. The tank was brought back to the shop. To join the union would be a problem because of our cash flow. We would have to join the union in order to ship the tank to Maui. The supplier was waiting for the tank. To join the union we had to be able to pay union benefits and dues for our men each month. We decided maybe a bank would give us a loan if we assigned the contract on the tank to them. We went to a bank for a loan and the loan was approved. We joined the union and our tank was shipped. It isn't easy to start and run a small business. We had to sacrifice a great deal of time and capital. Sometimes my paycheck went to pay for our men's union dues. As his company grew, we needed a larger shop. Frank found a larger shop and hired more men. He got a franchise for selling and putting up steel buildings and was contracted to put up several steel buildings for the government. It was his shop that fabricated the stainless steel railings leading into the Arizona Memorial at Pearl Harbor.

Sewage treatment tanks for the outside island hotels

Installing sewage tanks for The Sea Village

The company kept growing and needed even more room. My mother wanted to sell our condo and the beach property because Hawaii is a community property state. She was worried that if I died, Frank would have my share of these properties. I helped her sell them and we split the profits. Now Frank and I had the working capital needed to expand our business. There was a piece of property in an industrial center outside of the city. We bought this property and built our own shop. We were able to buy equipment that was needed. The shop was outside the city limits and our apartment was in the city. We decided to buy a house near the shop. We were able to acquire loans from the bank for the building of a shop and purchasing a house.

On weekends, we would head out with our dog to go fishing. We would start around 4:00 A.M. and take our 21 foot boat to go fishing in the Pacific Ocean. The boat was so small and the waves were so high that the waves would go over the boat or the boat would be on top of the waves.

I lived near the ocean all my life but never had time to learn to swim. Frank decided he wanted to learn to fly an airplane and he used his Veterans benefits to pay for lessons. I was so happy when he got his license. I hated the boat. He purchased a single engine airplane and later sold it for a twin engine. Of course the boat was sold. He would fly his men each morning to one of the outside islands and picked them up after work. This way we didn't have to pay for hotel expenses or pay each worker per day for staying over. Also, they would not be apart from their family for weeks. On weekends Frank, Buffy, (our dog) and I would fly to the outside islands.

First Airplane & co-pilot

Frank built his shop and the business grew. He had hired an administrator who also was the safety officer. He also had to hire a planning and estimator, a testing division manager (who had a certification from the Nuclear Regulatory Commission for the handling of radioactive isotopes used in radiographic testing) and a bookkeeper. It's hard to believe that Frank started this company alone, wearing a back brace, operating in a 600 sq. ft. shop with only $500. Yet the business made a gross of $24,000 in the first year. Just five short years later he built his own shop, 33,000 sq. ft. grossing $650,000. In August of 1977, one of Frank's welders was featured on the front cover of the weekly issue of the Builders Report Construction magazine. Inside was a 4 page article about our company, B & F Welding Inc. (**B**arbara & **F**rank Welding Inc.)

I was commuting to work by bus each day. It took me a little over an hour each way to get to work. One day when I returned home from work Frank said "Bobbie my bookkeeper gave her two weeks notice. She decided she wanted to move to the city. Why don't you quit your job and work for the company?" I thought it was a good idea and I would be working close to home. Two days later I gave the bank my notice. It wasn't easy. I worked for this bank for 16 years starting as a teller and working my way up to the position as Assistant Vice-President. I made sure that I told them I wasn't going to work for another bank. I was going to work with Frank. My friends said to me "You're going to be with your husband 24/7. You'll be back here". I never went back.

My mother and family started to speak to us. They were proud of us for our success. We both made trips to visit Frank's relatives in California. I remember the first time I met Frank's parents I was afraid they would not accept me. They were unlike my family. They immediately welcomed me into their family. Frank's father and younger brother came to spend their vacation with us. Everything was just great. After working for our company for three years disaster struck. A recession struck the islands. Economy in the island slowed down and it was difficult for us to bid and get jobs. Because of the recession companies were under bidding each other for whatever jobs they could find. We couldn't decide if we should shut down the business, sell what equipment we owned and voluntarily give up the shop property, vehicles, and our home. After much thought, we agreed it was in the best interest for us to close the business. Frank said "It is time for us to leave the islands". We would go to another state and start over. Other states had already gone through the recession. I asked him "Where will we go? We're not young anymore". We decided to go to California. He said "I know you love your family and you have been in these islands all your life. If you choose not to come with me I understand. However, if you should ever need me I'll always be there for you". I replied "I took a vow when I married you. It was for better or for worse, for richer or for poorer and in sickness and in health until death due us part. I'm coming with you". We sold whatever we owned and what we owed the bank we surrendered back to them. I couldn't understand how we had everything and lost it all. I asked "God, is your plan for us to have everything and then lose it all or do you have other plans for us?" I was depressed, angry and wanted to give up.

We said our goodbyes to our relatives and friends. It was hard to say goodbye to my mother. We had just started to get along with her. We moved to California where Frank's sister lived. We were unable to sell our airplane and paid someone to fly the plane to California. Our friends drove us to the airport. Before departing my friend said to me, "I'll always keep you in my prayers". The three of us, our dog Buffy, Frank and I were on our way to a new life in California. It took a great deal of courage for us to make a new life when we were in our early 50's.

CHAPTER FOUR
CALIFORNIA

When we arrived in California, Frank's sister, Shirley, and her husband let us stay with them. This gave us time to plan what we were going to do. Frank decided he wanted to start his own business. He applied for his California contractors' license and received his license. Now he had to buy a truck and tools. He was able to find a yard to store his tools. Shirley had a friend who owned a yard and they were willing to let Frank use it. We needed to find a house to rent. We stayed with Shirley for three months. To do all these things we needed money. We had some cash but it wasn't enough to purchase a truck. We were unable to sell the airplane. I couldn't ask my family for help but I had a good friend and we were friends since we were 18 years old. She and I worked at the same banks for 32 years and were friends all those years. I wrote to her and asked her if she could loan us $3500 for the purchase of a truck. A week or more later she mailed me a check for that amount. We lived

3000 miles away from her but she trusted us to pay her back. She could have written to me and said no. Again, God sent us help through our friend. I had lost faith and hope and this renewed my faith that He does care. Coming to California was part of His plan and perhaps all the adversities we endured in the islands made us stronger to start all over again.

Six months later I was able to find a job at a credit union. Frank started his one man company as a concrete contractor. He did small jobs. We were struggling but we hoped that we were heading in the right direction. We were able to sell the airplane and pay off my friend the money she lent us. He was able to hire a worker to help him and he did work for another contractor. Some of the work took him to Paso Robles which was 2 hours from Visalia. He had a lot of work in this city. He purchased a trailer and lived in a trailer park with Paco an African Gray parrot His sister gave him this bird to keep him company. He would come home to Visalia on week ends.

One day I had a call from a doctor at a hospital in the city Frank was working. He informed me that Frank had a heart attack. Shirley and her husband drove me to the hospital. We were told he had a mild heart attack and with medication he would be okay. He was released a few days afterwards. After his heart attack, we decided that it wasn't a good idea for him to be commuting each weekend and I should move to the city where he was working. I took time off from work to look for a job. I couldn't quit my job until I found another job. We both needed the health insurance. I went to several banks and received the same answer. I was overly qualified.

Several days after I got back home, the assistant manager of the credit union called me to her office. She said to me, "Barbara, were you able to find a job?" I told her no. Two days later she told me that she had gone to a conference and met another manager from a credit union in the county I wanted to move. She said, "I'll call him to see if he has any position for you. I don't think a husband and wife should live apart. If I were in the same position I would move". The next morning she told me she had called the manager and he wanted to set up an appointment for an interview. I went for the interview and was hired. I moved and Frank rented a house and a shop.

A year and a half later, he had another heart attack. I called an ambulance and the next day we were told that he needed a triple by-pass. I called my friend in the islands to please have her prayer group pray for us. The operation was successful. After staying at home a short time recuperating, he went back to work. He found a 10 acre parcel and wanted to build his own house and shop. His plan was we would live in a trailer and he would gradually build the house and shop.

**Frank putting up the entrance sign
for the area where we live**

The cost of the property was $40,000. We had the money to buy the property because the bank I worked for in the islands mailed me a check for my pension plan with them. I had forgotten about the plan. I had left the company after 16 years but had to leave the pension in there for 25 years. Also, we were able to pay off the Internal Revenue Service for the taxes our company owed when we left the islands. Paying this off cleared our credit. We decided that it was time for us to build the house and shop. We went to a bank to apply for a construction loan. The bank approved our loan. After the shop and house were built we applied for a mortgage loan. With hope, faith, hard work and prayers we were out of debt.

Just as we thought things would finally settle down the economy turned for the worse in the early 1990's. This would be the second recession that hit us. Many of our friends and workers left the state to relocate to other states. The first recession was in early 1980's and we were in our early 50's. Now 10 years later we were in our 60's. We weren't young anymore. It would be difficult for me to find another job and receive health insurance for us. Also, Frank would have to start a company in another state and apply for a state business license. After much discussion and thought, we decided to remain and wait for the economy to turn. Frank was able to hire men as he needed them. He had a few jobs that paid the bills and I was working. He did the foundations on two churches. A huge sign above the entrance to our home was done by him. I go through this entrance when I go to town. When I return home and just before I enter the entrance I look up and see Independence Ranch on the sign above the entrance. Then I realize although he is gone there are signs that he left behind. He did business with some great business people and through these people we were able to survive the economy until it turned around. They were two brothers who were developers and a father and son who owned a paving company.

Frank felt there was something wrong with his heart. He drove us to the hospital ER and before he checked in, he wanted one last cigarette. When the doctor asked him if had quit smoking, he said he had quit two weeks ago. He was admitted right then and had to have another triple by-pass on his heart. This time he was in Intensive Care for 10 days because he developed pneumonia. The surgery took seven hours. Again I called my friend in the islands to pray for us. The surgery was successful and he was able to go back to work. Throughout the years he was in and out of hospitals about fourteen times. He had four angioplasties done on his heart. He had a sore in his mouth which was cancerous. The doctor told him he had peripheral arterial disease in one of his legs. Surgery was done on his leg and mouth. The surgeries were successful. Frank was later told that he had diabetes. After many years of smoking, he finally quit. If he hadn't quit he would not have survived the last 29 years of his life.

Frank and I went back to the islands at least twice a year. He loved to travel. We would visit friends and relatives. On one occasion he said, "Bobbie why don't we visit the island you were raised on as a child?" The last time we were there was for my fathers' funeral. My father and I did not keep in touch with each other for 50 or more years. We did not write or call each other. Perhaps it was my fault because I was filled with anger and hate because he had left my mother and me. I did not make any attempt to get in touch with him. I could never forgive him for leaving us. When we arrived on the island, we went to the cemetery where he was buried and I asked for forgiveness. The anger and hate that I carried for 50 years or longer was gone. I felt a certain peace within myself. Also, while I was there I met my half-sister for the first time. I told her how I envied her because she had both parents. She said, "I had both parents for a short while. My mother left our father to live in California where I was born. She later brought me back to live with him". My half-sister lived with her Auntie for a time because our father could not raise a young child by himself. She said he later remarried and her step-mother was a very nice woman. My half-sister is 10 years younger than me. I'm glad that we had finally met each other. Today, we are friends although we live 3000 miles apart we keep in touch.

One day I received a call from my cousin who informed me that my mother was ill. I went back to see her. Upon my arrival I immediately took her to the emergency hospital. I was told she had suffered a mild stroke. She was hospitalized for two days and released. Also, I was told she could no longer live alone. I called Frank to let him know she could no longer live alone. He said, "Let her know we will take care of her. She can come to live with us in California or you can find her an assisted living facility in the islands". My mother decided to come live with us in California. I packed her belongings and we left for California. While we worked I hired someone to stay with her during the day. She lived with us for 6 years. During these years she came to know and love Frank.

One day the caregiver had to leave early and no one was home with her. One of our neighbors found her walking. She told them she was going to Honolulu. They kept her at their home until we got home from work. We decided that it was time for us to place her in a care facility. It was a very difficult thing to do.

We found a real nice care home. She had only been there for two weeks and I received a call. They said I would have to find another facility for her. I asked them what happened. I was told that my mother had said, "We are going on a strike". My mother was 93 years old and had dementia. I thought it was easy to find another care home for her. I found out it was not easy. I called several homes and they said they would call me back. I never got calls so I called them. I was told they were unable to accommodate us. I told someone I could not find my mother another care home. She suggested that I call an organization called Ombudsmen. I called and they sent someone to meet me at the care facility. We both went to talk to the director of the home. She let them know it was too soon to evaluate my mother. Two weeks was not enough time to evaluate anyone. They agreed to re-evaluate her in a month. After the month was over I received a call from the home. They had made a mistake by wanting her to leave. The director of the home said to me, "She was a sweet lady and didn't require much help". My mother remained at the home until she died a year and a half later.

In 2007 the country was in another recession. We were now in our 70's. After I retired from the credit union, Frank said, "I'm going to close the business. I think this recession will take longer than the other two. At our age we can't afford to use our savings or refinance our home to keep the business". I agreed with him. It was difficult for him to lay off his employees however, it was the right decision. We made several trips to Honolulu and enjoyed our retirement.

One early morning after two years of retirement, I heard Frank call me. He could hardly speak. He was at his computer. He said, "I'm having a difficult time with reading the words on the computer. I think I'm having a stroke." I said to him, "Let me call the doctor." He replied, "Let's wait and see if my speech will come back". By noon time he was still having a difficult time. It was Sunday. I tried calling his doctor but got another doctor that was on duty. I told the doctor what was happening and he told me we needed to call a neurologist and hung up the phone. I had a friend in Honolulu whose brother had a stroke. I called her and asked her what symptoms her brother had when he had his stroke. I told her I thought Frank had a stroke. He was unable to form words or read and had a difficult time speaking. She immediately told me to hang up and call for an ambulance. As soon as I hung up the phone, the doctor called back and told me to take Frank to the ER.

It was late Sunday afternoon when we arrived at the hospital. They ran several tests on him. We were told he had a minor stroke and had to remain in the hospital. The next morning I went to the hospital. I was surprised he was up and he got his speech back. His carotid artery on the left side of his neck was 90% to 95% clogged. The right side was 80% to 85% clogged. Also, an artery in his heart where an angioplasty was done 20 years ago was clogged. His heart had to be regulated before any operation could be performed. When his heart was regulated, the doctors decided to first take care of his heart problem. An angioplasty was done on his heart and he was released the next day. The doctors decided to wait before they operated on his carotid artery. Two months later the surgery was performed. The operation was successful and after four days in the hospital he was released. I called my friends to thank them for their prayers.

Two months after the surgery on his carotid artery, he complained about pains in his stomach. We went to see our doctor on Monday. Tests were done on him Tuesday, Wednesday and Thursday. Late Thursday I called our doctor to find out about the tests. The doctor said, "I don't have good news. He has tumors in his stomach and they have metastasized. Two things can be done. We can send him for chemotherapy and in two months he would be gone or we can just wait". I couldn't believe what I was hearing. I replied, "Are you saying to me that Frank is dying". The doctor said, "I want to talk to you both. I would like to see you both in my office tomorrow". Every three months the doctor would have Frank come in for a check up and get blood work done. These tumors were never detected. I asked myself why now. Perhaps these tumors were not detected for a reason. After he died, I did not want an autopsy to be done to find out if they were cancerous. In my heart I knew the tumors were cancerous.

I remembered what a business friend of Frank said to me, "If you ever get cancer or know of anyone, I know of a good oncologist". I immediately called him. It was close to 5:00 P.M. I told him Frank had tumors in his stomach and I needed a doctor. He said he would get in touch with the doctor and would call me. Later he called me to let me know he had contacted the doctor and we had an appointment for Friday. I told him we had an early appointment to see our doctor. He said, "When you get through, call me and I'll be waiting for you and Frank to see the oncologist". I said, "What time is our appointment?" He said, "The doctor will see Frank as soon as you get to his office. No appointment is necessary. I will be waiting for both of you."

We arrived at our doctor's office. He suggested that we see an oncologist. I told him we had an appointment with one. We left his office to meet our friend at the oncologist's office. After the oncologist examined Frank he told us to take him to the hospital. It was noon time when we arrived and Frank was admitted. Meanwhile our friend stayed with me until the doctor came in and spoke to us. She told us on Saturday tests would be done to see if the tumors were cancerous. When we left I told Frank that I would see him the next day. He nodded his head. I never thought this would be our last time together. Later that Friday night at 10:15 P.M I received a call from the hospital. I was told to come to the hospital as soon as possible. They didn't think he would make it through the night. I called our friend to ask if he would take me to the hospital. I explained to him the hospital called and said that Frank would not make it through the night. He came to pick me up. I felt bad asking him to drive me back to the hospital. He had been with us all day Friday.

We arrived at the hospital before mid-night. When I saw Frank in the hospital bed, I couldn't believe he was dying. I saw the monitor going up and down. Suddenly it went silent and he was gone. How could this happen. I couldn't cry because I could not believe he was gone. I didn't have any warning and couldn't call my friends for prayers.

This was a bad dream and I would wake up. He drove himself on Thursday to the pathology lab. He went to the hospital Friday afternoon and in 14 hours he was gone. This isn't happening. He had gone in and out of hospitals fourteen times during our 39 years of marriage and he would always return home and go back to work in a day or two. I said to myself I'll wake up from this bad dream and everything will be fine. This never happened.

We left the hospital and the next day when I woke up I was still in shock. Friends helped me with all the funeral arrangements. I went through the motion of living each day in shock. I didn't want to get up in the mornings. One of my dogs got sick and I had to take him the vet. The vet had lost her husband a year ago and knew about the grief and pain of losing a spouse. She told me about a hospice support group that helped her through her grief. After four weeks, I decided I needed help and attended this group. I was there physically but my mind was elsewhere. I attended these weekly meetings for several months before I realized Frank was gone. He wasn't coming back and I must work on my grief and pain. At these meetings I met others who were experiencing the same grief and pain. To deal with grief is very difficult. Losing a spouse, child, family member, friend or a pet is painful. The pain never goes away. At this group I found some peace and friends. Also, at church I found hope, faith and trust in God. I was left behind for a purpose. I found a certain peace knowing that Frank went so quickly and peacefully. He didn't suffer like so many other patients who had cancer. Frank was talking to us on the way to the hospital and he was awake when we left him in the evening.

This would be unlike the other fourteen times he had been in and out of hospitals and returned home. He had no idea until that same day he was admitted to the hospital that he had tumors in his stomach. It took me awhile before I realized how difficult it would have been for him to have cancer treatments. Even with treatments he would eventual die because the tumors were through out his stomach organs. He was a strong individual and would not like to have been a burden to anyone.

Like many of you often I had thoughts of what ifs in my life. One of them was what if my grandfather had never left China and was afraid to attempt to leave his country to come to a strange land. My family and I would not be here and I would not be writing this story. Another what if is Frank had not told mother he was going to ask me to marry him and she had not told me if I did to move out from her condo. What if I had just walked past and not gone into the Lady of Peace Cathedral for answers to my problem. I would not have met Frank. Perhaps we are here to fulfill a purpose. God has a plan for each one of us. He had a plan for my grandfather filled with hope and faith when he got on that steamship to come to America. I followed His plan when Frank had told me that if I preferred I could remain in the islands and not leave my family and the islands to start a new life in California. I left the islands and my family filled with hope and faith to a new location. The moment I meet Frank God had plans for both of us.

As I'm writing my story, I look back and see how God has put so many wonderful people in our lives. They have touched us with their presence. Life is never easy. We must believe in something because life is too hard to go through alone. My family had hardships, financial, mental, and physical. They never gave up. The economy maybe bad and we lose our homes, jobs or unable to find a job, however, we can hope for better times. As long as we are here we will have hardships as well as joyous moments. Just remember this is a journey we must all take until eternity. There are no exceptions. Perhaps I'm here to write or share my story to give hope to others who are hurting and to relieve my own pain and grief. I don't know the reasons why bad things happen to good people. I know disasters and obstacles made me a stronger person. I'm sure He knows and will show us the way. I know sometimes I feel I'm alone but I know I'm never alone because He walks with me and will carry me if I can't walk. There are angels here on earth and He puts them in our lives to help each other. At the moment we may not recognize them but they are in our midst.

I call these angels on earth my earth angels. My earth angels have been a blessing in my life and I hope I can return their blessings to others.

Like many of you, I think about the past and worry about my future. The past is gone and I may never see the future. I must live in the present – now - and live one day at a time in the best way I know. Though I know the pain of losing a loved one will never go away but with hope, faith and friends I know I can move on through the hard times and well as the joyous times.